Thoughts Along the Journey

Thoughts Along the Journey

Reflections on Being a Christian

Robert W. Janek

FOREST OF PEACE
Publishing

Suppliers for the Spiritual Pilgrim
Leavenworth, KS

Thoughts Along the Journey

Library of Congress Cataloging-in-Publication Data

Janek, Robert W. , 1941-
Thoughts along the journey : reflections on being a Christian / Robert W. Janek
p. cm.
Includes bibliographical references.
ISBN 0-939516-39-X
1. Christian life—Unity of the Brethren authors. 2. Janek, Robert W., 1941- . I. Title.
BV4501.2.J334 1998
248.4'846—dc21 97-49695
CIP

published by

Forest of Peace Publishing, Inc.
PO Box 269
Leavenworth, KS 66048-0269 USA
1-800-659-3227

printed by
Hall Directory, Inc.
Topeka, KS 66608-0348

1st printing: January 1998

Images from *Woodcut Manual* (1932), by J.J. Lankes, courtesy of www.arttoday.com

Dedicated
to

my mother,
Eda Lisso Janek,
through whose love
this spiritual journey
has been made possible

The earthy goal
of the journey toward God
is not to find him
in some blinding,
beatific experience,
but to struggle ceaselessly
to continue the journey.

– John Shea
The Critic

Contents

Preface

Several years ago, I began writing short articles for a monthly newspaper that was published by the medical center where I am a staff chaplain. The articles are what I call mental meanderings or personal musings (in Webster's terms, "to turn something over in the mind meditatively, and often inconclusively"). They are the "inconclusive" reflections of one particular human being on a life-journey, which has been, at least in part, influenced and guided by my personal, and probably unique, understanding of what it means to be a Christian. As with any human journey through life, these pages reflect different and changing or evolving perspectives and observations along the road I travel. Like all roads, the scenery along my journey changes from day to day, month to month and year to year; and consequently, so do my perspectives on an understanding of life, myself, God and what it means to be a Christian and a spiritual pilgrim.

More recently, at the urging of a minister friend of mine, many of these articles have been published in the *Brethren Journal*, a monthly magazine of the Unity of the Brethren, a small Protestant denomination in Texas in which lie many of my spiritual and religious roots.

I invite the reader of this collection of thoughts not so much to analyze or critique my personal musings or my life story (each of our stories is unique), as to use these reflections and observations to reflect on her or his own life-journey, and hopefully, in some small way, to enrich the reader's own life.

Variations on the Theme of the New Year

In talking about the changing of the years, Eugene Kennedy, in his book *The Joy of Being Human*, observed:

> We are usually glad to see the old year go—although its scars remain—but we are happy to have another chance at being or doing better. Most of us are like that, thank God, and, even as we climb out of the wreckage of the year past, we want to try again at doing the right thing about ourselves, our work, and our neighbor. The new year makes us think old thoughts about who we are and what we might become; it is a time to think about our promises even as we remember our failings—an interval for hope rather than regrets.[1]

Sometimes, I suspect that if there were not an occasion called the New Year, we, as hoping beings, would have to invent one. We almost *need* a New Year, a time in which we can feel the opportunity to start all over, to make amends for past errors and wrong turns, to attempt to get back on the right track, to rejuvenate our energy. We almost *need* a break in time, between the old and the new; between the past, present and future. We need a break in time to give us hope, in which we can get a second chance, or a third, or fourth, or even a ten-thousandth chance!

The Psalmist in the Old Testament wrote: "Weeping may tarry for the night, but joy comes with the morning." The turning of the calendar, the New Year, is often like the arrival of that Psalmist's morning: a time for joy and hope.

We have the possibility to put the dusty, broken past behind us and to look to a new day. The New Year can renew within us a sense of hope that our past misdeeds and sins and failures and broken dreams and wrong turns need not weigh us down. They need not destroy our future. The New Year can renew within us hope that even many of our most crushing experiences, those heretofore deemed wasted or useless, can be redeemed. They can be turned into lessons by which we can positively and creatively contribute to making life a little more livable for others (and consequently, for ourselves).

The New Year is one of those times, which also include anniversary dates and the season of autumn, when we become most aware of the movement of time. It thus becomes an opportunity for spiritual renewal, an occasion to ask some questions of ourselves: "Where have I been thus far in my life-journey?"... "Where am I now?"... "Where am I going?" (Often, I think that the direction we are headed in life is more important than where we have been or where we are at any given moment!)... "What are the values, goals and priorities that influence my direction?"... "How have I measured 'success' and 'failure' in my life—and are there perhaps other ways of evaluating my progress that would make my life more rewarding, worthwhile and meaningful?" ... "What is most important in life; that is, what has given my life meaning and a sense of purpose?"... "Who have been the most important and influential people in my life: those persons who have encouraged me when I felt no courage; those persons who, through their actions and/or words, let me know that I am someone special; those persons who have reached out to me when others were turning away or had given up on me; those persons who have pointed out to me my talents and gifts; those persons who have accepted me in spite of my faults rather than criticizing and judging me for those shortcomings?"

Our responses to these kinds of questions can help us set new directions, new priorities, new goals. They can provide new and more hopeful perspectives as we continue our journeys into the New Year.

The Griefs That We Bear

The new year is not only a time of rejoicing and celebration—a kind of built-in chance to start all over, to change directions, to create new goals, to make amends, to renew hope that *this* year will be better than the last year, maybe even a chance to forgive oneself—but there is also a certain sadness in this season. New beginnings are also old endings, and old endings most often are a time of grief, great or small, even as we look forward with excitement and anticipation to a new beginning. The sadness is because the changing of the years is one of those times when we are most aware of what Loren Eiseley calls "time's arrow"[2]: another year of our life, and of our loved ones, is behind us. Further, as we reflect on the past year, we remember (however briefly) the losses as well as the gains that occurred.

Loss and the consequent grief (no matter how mild or severe) is integral to the human condition. We all experience many losses in life, even though many of these losses are not recognized as such. There are the obvious losses, like death and divorce, losing a job or a house or a car, but there are also other kinds of losses which are not so obvious. Still, they are very real: the loss of self-esteem, of innocence, of hope, of self-respect, of ideals and goals, of enthusiasm for living, of a sense of purpose or meaning in life, of faith and trust—to name just a few. We grieve these losses too.

I do not believe that we ever get over our losses—not after a year, not after two years, never. Grief, as I see it, is a kind of psycho-spiritual rock within us. Initially it has sharp and jagged edges that can be painful, cutting and tearing at our very being, even at our desire to keep on living. Gradually, over the days and weeks and months and years, like a rock tumbling down a flowing river, it smooths out, but it never disappears. The loss becomes a part of who we are as a human person, affecting the way we see, understand, interpret and relate to the world we encounter.

Further, as I continue to journey through life, I am more and more aware that there are two kinds of experiences of loss: a sudden awareness and a gradually increasing awareness.

We are well acquainted with a sudden experience. Such losses as the loss of a loved one or the loss of a ball game are usually focused on a specific, concrete event to which we can point.

The gradually-increasing-awareness-of-loss experience is much more subtle, yet just as real. It also can be just as painful when it reaches its greatest intensity. Instead of being a specific event, this kind of loss is a process spread over time. This kind of loss, and the resulting grief, does not hit us suddenly. It begins quietly and gradually like the distant thunder of an approaching storm and grows in intensity as we become more and more aware that what we had hoped for or planned for or assumed or envisioned will never come about. We might, for example, suffer an increasing awareness over time that we will never be married or that we will never have the children we once dreamed of having, or that we will never be the person we thought we would turn out to be or that we will not become the company CEO, a position we had been working toward for years, or that we will not accomplish all that we set out to accomplish. This kind of growing awareness of loss can also come in the form of an increasing realization that loved ones will not be around forever, that we will sooner or later experience their loss. This realization, in turn, can lead to anticipatory grief, that anguish we feel at an expected loss.

In this, I believe that we Christians can strive to be aware of and sensitive to the many and varied kinds of losses that people, including ourselves, experience throughout life—and the grief that accompanies those losses—so that we can be present with and available to those who are hurting. This presence, this availability, is most often manifested through a caring, trustworthy, understanding attitude toward others, an attitude which invites and encourages others to feel at ease in sharing their hurts with us. As Christians, we can thus acknowledge others' losses as being real to them just as ours are to us. Such support can help us be, in the words of Psalm 46, "a very present help" to others in the griefs that they bear.

Thinking About "Thinking Christian"

Many years ago, I went through a kind of personal mental exercise of attempting to understand what it means to be a Christian in everyday life. I finally came to the conclusion that it has to do with how a person thinks about things. It has to do with a person's attitude toward self, toward others, toward the nonhuman part of creation, toward God. It has to do with a different way of seeing things, a different way of understanding and interpreting personal experiences, a different way of reacting to life and what life hands us. I call this process "thinking Christian."

Among other things, this kind of thinking means being honest with ourselves in that we don't always look elsewhere to find fault or make excuses for how things happen. Instead, we are willing to admit that sometimes *we* bring about our own problems. We are willing to accept responsibility for our own actions and decisions, not pushing the blame off onto someone else. On the other hand, it also involves the ability to see that we do not need to accept the blame for all the world's ills, causing us to be weighed down by a paralyzing sense of guilt. There is a balance, and I suspect that this balance has to do with the idea of humility, recognizing our strengths, abilities and talents as well as our weaknesses and failings, recognizing that each of us has something positive and creative to offer life, recognizing that in spite of all the flaws and failings we can see within ourselves each of us is a worthwhile creation of God, recognizing that in spite of our sinfulness God can use us. As God used the very human Abraham and Moses and David and Ruth and Jeremiah and Amos and Paul and Peter, so God can also use us in God's work here on earth. This work of God is struggling to love and care for and about others, making life a little more livable.

Such humility is really a radical form of honesty (I call it brutal honesty). It has to do with being in touch with our feelings—our anger, our loneliness, our fears and anxieties, our joys and sorrows—yet accepting them as a real God-given part of who we are without believing that we must somehow hide them or deny having them in the name of a strong faith.

"Thinking Christian" also means recognizing that even the greatest and most successful among us struggle with various burdens in life. It means being aware that all of us are struggling to feel good about ourselves, struggling to feel that we are worthwhile human beings, that we are not part of some cosmic mistake but have legitimacy and value as individuals. This recognition leads to exercising patience with others, to appreciating and understanding the life-experience of others, as we struggle to be a part of the solution and not part of the problem.

"Thinking Christian" has to do with our attitude toward others. It means cultivating an attitude of reconciliation and forgiveness rather than an attitude of judgment and condemnation, an attitude of acceptance rather than suspicion and rejection. It means seeing others as fellow travellers, not as objects to be manipulated and exploited for our own selfish ends. It means striving to bring out the best in others, relating to others in ways that encourage the best that is within them (their divine nature?) rather than deliberately bringing out the worst or playing upon their weaknesses. It means being eager to learn, being open-minded, realizing that we can always learn more and expand our horizons.

"Thinking Christian" means realizing that ultimately God (not necessarily society) measures a person's success in life not by how popular or wealthy or intelligent or powerful or attractive or cunning that person is, but by how loving and caring. It means realizing that we are all different, with unique talents and abilities and qualities which can be used to make this world a better place.

"Thinking Christian" also has to do with how we relate to the world around us—to the environment, to the nonhuman part of God's creation. It means sensing the sacred in the seemingly ordinary (perhaps God does not separate the world into the sacred and secular as do humans). It means feeling a sense of responsibility toward the environment, realizing that we humans possess the frightening freedom and the power to adversely affect it, that God has given us the freedom to exploit it into oblivion or to nurture it into continuing healthiness.

I don't believe that one begins to "think Christian" overnight (although there may be certain experiences which trigger immediate insight and illumination). Instead, it is a gradual process of expanding awareness, appreciation, understanding and sensitivity.

"Thinking Christian" is a lifelong process, a journey of personal growth. We never arrive at some ideal point but are always growing, always becoming. There will be times when we are painfully aware that we have failed to live up to the standards we believe God has set for us, yet, ironically, "thinking Christian" means that we realize God wants us to get up and continue the journey. We realize that God does not want us so weighed down by guilt and shame and a sense of failure that we become paralyzed and cannot move on in our journey. "Thinking Christian" means realizing that God is more interested in what kind of person we are becoming than in what kind of person we have been. Thus, for one who "thinks Christian" there is always hope.

Reconciliation

On the night of November 15, 1940, the Nazis bombed and destroyed one of the great cathedrals of England in Coventry. As officials considered reconstruction, they decided not to build on the same location, but instead constructed a new and much more modern cathedral next to the burned-out shell of the old one. The new cathedral would be connected to the ruins of the old one by a high-ceilinged porch.

Within the remains of the destroyed cathedral is a statue, given in 1995, fifty years after the war. It is titled "Reconciliation." As I stood there in the summer of 1996 looking at that statue of a kneeling man and woman embracing in the midst of all that destruction, I was overcome with emotion. It was a most powerful symbol of humans' struggle to relate to each other in love and compassion and forgiveness. (I keep an enlarged photograph in my office to remind me of what being a Christian is all about!)

In his book *The Humility of God*, John MacQuarrie wrote:

> Reconciliation means a deep change in the relations between two people or groups of people, a change in which enmity and alienation are replaced by peace and mutual acceptance.[3]

Reconciliation is much easier spoken of than lived out, especially if I believe that I am the one who was wronged! It's something I personally struggle with.

How can reconciliation between two people or groups of people come about? Perhaps by recognizing our own humanity (or what I call "humanness"). Perhaps by realizing that we too "have sinned and fall short of the glory of God," that perhaps we are also a part of the problem, that we did or said something that contributed to the other person reacting the way she or he did.

Part of the great emotional power of the statue is that we can easily imagine that somehow these two people have been wounded by life, perhaps by human relationships, and that they have suddenly realized how they have played a part in the wounding. We can gaze upon that statue and imagine that perhaps one of these people, who normally cared deeply for the other, has hurt that one, and, in this kneeling embrace, they are now trying to put life back together, to forgive and be forgiven.

How can reconciliation, this "deep change in the relations between two people or groups of people," come about? Perhaps by reinterpreting the other's actions or words or motives. From this new perspective we might see how something we said or did innocently or in jest touched a deeply painful place in the other person, leading that person to react in anger and hurt. Or we might see how we felt hurt or rejected or snubbed by what we thought were the deliberate actions or words of another person toward us that may not have been intentionally harmful. We might recognize that a silence or break in communications between us and another person which we interpreted as malicious may not have been deliberately so. Thus, if we can stop and reflect, we begin to realize that our interpretation may be wrong, that the other person meant no harm.

How can reconciliation—"a change in which enmity and alienation are replaced by peace and mutual acceptance"—come about? Perhaps, in times of tension and alienation, *we* need to overcome our own anger and bitterness, our own feeling of woundedness, our own feeling of self-pity and the feeling of having been the victim of injustice, and take the initiative toward healing the wounds of human relationships. Sometimes, the other person is more severely wounded than we are—and we don't realize it—and that person doesn't have the strength or energy to reach out to us in reconciliation. Or that person may not know how, or may fear being hurt even more, or may feel too much guilt or shame, or may believe that *we* should take the initiative toward reconciliation. One of the beautiful aspects of this statue is that *both* people are on their knees. There is no sense of moral or spiritual superiority: Both have been wounded by life, both are feeling their humanness, both are feeling their need to forgive and be forgiven, to understand and to be understood, to love and to be loved.

How can reconciliation come about? Perhaps the incentive for reconciliation comes about when we begin to realize that without it tensions will continue, that anger and alienation and distrust will only increase, ending or destroying the relationship. Perhaps we struggle to reconcile our differences when we begin to realize that without reconciliation there is a kind of spiritual cancer that eats away at us and can destroy our own integrity, our true sense of self-worth. Such a spiritual cancer can make us much less than God intended us to be as human beings and can bring out our mean-spiritedness, our dark side. Realizing that unreconciled relationships, either between individuals or groups, wound all involved, perhaps we can all keep a place in our hearts for an image of that statue in the destroyed cathedral in Coventry.

Encountering the Potholes of Life

Some time ago, a patient and I were discussing the weather (a politically safe subject in Kansas), especially the possibility of spring and summer thunderstorms and tornadoes. At one point when I indicated a concern about tornadoes, he reacted by saying that as a person with (divine) connections, why should I worry? God would protect me. This triggered many thoughts.

First, I do not believe that God protects certain favorite people while allowing others to suffer. I think that Jesus was attempting to point this out in the

Sermon on the Mount when he observed: ". . . He (God) makes His sun rise on the evil and on the good, and sends rain on the just and on the unjust" (Mt. 5: 45). I personally do not believe that being an ordained minister, or even a Christian, exempts me from the painful side of the human condition, even the effects of tornadoes, if I don't use what little God-given intelligence I possess to get out of the way!

Second, I do not believe that as an ordained minister I am any better, spiritually superior, more special or more worth protecting in the eyes of God than anyone else. In this, I very much appreciate Peter's reaction to Cornelius when he fell down at Peter's feet and worshipped him: "Stand up; I too am a man" (Acts 10: 25-26).

These thoughts sent me scurrying to files of clippings, articles and notes that I had accumulated over the years, where I found a list of other things to think about as we travel down the road of life. They were put together by a minister in Canada, Rev. Cornie G. Remple. I list them, with a few comments and observations of my own.

(1) "Suffering is not God's desire for us, but occurs in the process of life."[4]

God seems to have created a world in which tornadoes and floods and droughts and hurricanes and earthquakes occur—and has given us humans the freedom to kill each other in war and murder and accident. I suspect that if we realize at least some suffering is going to be a normal part of life, we will be better able to deal with it creatively or redemptively when it occurs, that we will be able to use it as an occasion to contribute to life.

(2) "Suffering is not given in order to teach us something, but through it we learn."

I would make a slight, but I believe, significant

change in this: "Suffering is not given in order to teach us something but through it we *have the opportunity to learn.*" I don't think that we automatically learn from suffering, that we automatically learn something that is contributive to society and to ourselves.

I had polio as a child, but never did I believe that somehow God had deliberately given it to me to teach me something. However, I *do* hope that I have learned compassion and understanding through that experience!

An acquaintance of mine once told me how she became more aware of and sensitive to the suffering of others through her own suffering: She had learned through her personal suffering. Immediately after the breakup of a promising relationship, her inner pain was so intense that she felt compelled to flee, to get away by herself. She drove up to the Red Rocks area in the foothills of the Rocky Mountains overlooking the city of Denver. As she gazed at the vast expanse of the city that stretched before her, she began to be aware of the terrible pain that must be happening all over Denver at that very moment. People were confronting illness, loneliness, divorce, loss of a job, abuse, death, grief—the list would be endless. Her center of attention shifted from her own woundedness, and her entire mood and perspective became transformed. Somehow, deep within her, she felt an empathy with all of those who were also hurting, even though their particular circumstances might be different. Her heart reached out to them as she sat among the rocks. She wanted to help them in some way, to find a way to ease their pain. As she travelled back toward Denver in the twilight of that memorable day, the fierce fire of her own searing pain had been extinguished. She felt calmed and returned to an inner balance. Even more than that, she had grown, she had deepened. Her personal sense of significance, purpose and mission had been reaffirmed. Years later as she reflected on this experience, she told me that it was nothing less "than the spirit of God's love at work with her among the Red Rocks."

(3) "Suffering is not given to us to teach others something, but through it they may learn."

To think that God would make one person suffer in order to teach another person something would, I believe, be to see God as cruel and unjust. While I don't believe that God gave me polio when I was eleven years old in order to teach my parents something, I'm sure that they learned from it!

(4) "Suffering is not given to punish us, but it is sometimes the consequence of sin or poor judgment."

First, I understand sin to be personal and/or corporate attitudes which lead to destructive acts. For example, personal insecurity can lead to greed, which, in turn, can lead to the exploitation of others and to the wasteful use of natural resources. In human relationships, low self-esteem can lead to a need to denigrate others in an effort to feel better about oneself. Thus, our sins can cause great suffering, but that suffering is the natural consequence of our attitudes and actions and not deliberate punishment by God!

Further, suffering caused by poor judgment is not deliberate punishment from God! A person driving down a winding gravel road in the middle of the night at 90 miles an hour should not interpret the wreck that occurs as punishment by God but as horribly poor judgment on his or her part.

(5) "Suffering does not occur because our faith is weak, but through suffering our faith may be strengthened."

Suffering can force us to reexamine our image of God and our understanding of how God works in our lives, thus making our faith more mature and more relevant to the human condition. For example, suffering may force us to give up the image of God as a bribable guarantor against pain and suffering and adopt a more relevant image of God as One who helps us through pain and suffering.

Further, those who say that suffering is due to weak faith do not take into consideration the examples of many, many people of great faith throughout the history of Christianity who suffered at the hands of others, not because of weak faith but because of an especially *strong* faith.

(6) "God does not depend upon human suffering to achieve God's purposes, but through suffering God's purposes are sometimes achieved."

When the suffering of others, or our own suffering, leads to compassionate understanding, to advances in medical technology, to better tornado detection systems, to ways to avoid wars, to a more sympathetic appreciation for our environment, etc., then the suffering has contributed to some of God's purposes.

(7) "Suffering is not always to be avoided at all costs, but sometimes is chosen."

Sometimes suffering (or the potential for suffering) is deliberately chosen. For example, a person, out of a sense of patriotism, may volunteer to fight for her/his nation. Another person, out of that same sense of (but different interpretation of) patriotism, may flee to another country to avoid fighting what he/she perceives as an unjust war (as did many during the Viet Nam conflict). In either case a set of principles leads to a choice that will hold a particular kind of suffering.

(8) "Suffering can either destroy us or add meaning to life."

I personally find that suffering is extremely neutral

in that it can make us more sensitive and caring and appreciative of others, or it can harden us, making us insensitive and cynical. We can grow from it, or we can be diminished by it. It is not an automatically guaranteed learning and growth experience!

(9) "The will of God has more to do with how we respond to life, than how life deals with us."

It's not so much what happens to us but how we handle what happens to us that counts in life. There are times when we cannot control what happens to us, but we *do* have some control over how we react to what happens to us. For instance, I could not help having polio and the consequent facial paralysis, but I have always had some control over how I respond to that experience!

Perhaps we can reorient our thinking from believing that God deliberately brings about suffering to seeing how God helps us *through* suffering.

As Harvey Potthoff observed:

> God is present in adversity as that reality in the light of which experiences which have been counted as wasted, evil, or tragic may be gathered into some new pattern of meaning, purpose and wholeness. The reality of God is mediated by persons who reveal that adversity can be redemptive.[5]

Easter: A Fresh Perspective

In *A Theology of the Living Church*, L. Harold DeWolf wrote of Easter:

> This man who was despised, condemned, tortured and killed by sinful men represented the Father's own will as no other had ever done. In condemning Jesus, men were condemning the purpose of God. How would God respond to this clearest, most unequivocal outburst of human rebellion? It is His own purpose which has guided His faithful Son and brought him into this suffering. Now what will the Father do? Will He send lightning or earthquake to destroy the wretched sinners who have presumed to attack His Son? Not if He is truly the Father who has been faithfully represented by the teaching and life of Jesus. If He is such a Father He may send an ominous darkness over Calvary which men will later recall as the symbol of His withholding the power He possessed to stop or punish them. But he will not contradict the love revealed through Christ by striking down the sinners in wrathful power. He will wait behind the shadows, suffering in such agony as might be guessed at by a human parent who has been compelled to stand by while his child is tortured to death, but such as only the God who is perfect in understanding love and who loves the torturers too can fully know. He will let sin have its way that sinners may know its meaning through to its fulfillment and that they may learn also the love of God.[6]

I'm intrigued by DeWolf's observation about the meaning and significance of the Easter story. If my understanding of what he is attempting to say is correct, perhaps there is another way of understanding or interpreting the Easter experience. That is, Easter is such a profound and hopeful occasion not because it is about Jesus being some kind of substitute or sacrifice for our sins (and then God snatching him from the jaws of death) but because that event reveals, as no other could, the true nature of a God whose love overwhelms our humanity!

In one sense, the world hesitated for those three days, holding its breath: "What would this God do to people who had crucified His son?" As DeWolf asks: "Will He send lightning or earthquake to destroy the wretched sinners who have presumed to attack His son?" Perhaps that is what other gods of the ancients would have done—and the people of that time were very much aware of other religious beliefs! We know what we would likely do if we had been forced to watch a loved one being tortured and then executed. I expect that every bone in our body would cry out for justice, and we would be tempted to seek self-righteous revenge against those who had done such a cruel deed! However, this God proved to be radically different! This God did *not* punish the perpetrators! Again, in DeWolf's words:

> But He will not contradict the love revealed through Christ by striking down the sinners in wrathful power. He will wait behind the shadows, suffering in such agony as might be guessed at by a human parent who had been compelled to stand by while his child is tortured to death, but such as only the God who is perfect in understanding love and who loves the torturers too can fully know.[6]

However, this kind of sacrificial, unconditional love seems too hard, and perhaps too disturbing, to understand. Perhaps we don't even *want* to understand it because such all-giving, infinitely forgiving love is far beyond our human capacities. Perhaps we don't *want* to believe in such unconditional love because when *we* are hurt in some way, we tend to lash out in anger and vengeance, attempting to punish the perpetrator (or the most available target). Often, we have to vent our rage before we can even think of forgiveness! Furthermore, we want our God to be the same way, especially when we feel we have been wronged! I suspect that we humans all too often let our own desire for vengeance, our own anger and vindictiveness, our own felt need to get even, our own need to punish those who threaten or hurt us, distort our understanding of the nature of God.

Perhaps it could be said that God realized at the time, and realizes now, that to seek revenge would be to stoop to the lowest human level of thinking and acting. For God to exact revenge, to get even, to punish the perpetrators, would be to defeat God's own message of unlimited, unconditional, sacrificial love. It would be to undermine the message that only this kind of love can ultimately save humanity from destroying itself.

I suggest that we see glimpses of this higher way of existing and thinking—of loving and acting—in passages such as Isaiah 55: 8-9:

> For my thoughts are not your thoughts, neither are your ways my ways, says the Lord. For as the heavens are higher than the earth, so are my ways higher than your ways and my thoughts than your thoughts.

And in Hosea 11: 9:

> I will not execute my fierce anger, I will not again

> destroy Ephraim; for I am God and not man, the Holy One in your midst, and I will not come to destroy.

Thus, I risk suggesting that Easter is not so much about Christ dying in some kind of atonement or substitute or sacrifice for our sinfulness as it is about a God whose love for creation is so great that it overcomes our sinfulness! Easter is an expression of a love so overwhelming that we feel a great sense of guilt and shame and self-judgment when we realize that we have betrayed that love (not unlike what Judas and Peter must have felt when they realized what they had done to the very person who loved them unconditionally). It is not unlike the agony we feel when we fail or betray one who loves us. Yet this same love forgives our betrayal and our human shortcomings, and encourages us to "rise and walk!"

> He will let sin have its way that sinners may know its meaning all the way through to its fulfillment and that they may learn also the love of God.[6]

It Starts with Easter

If there is a biblical heart to my personal journey of faith, a journey of not one but a thousand new births, it would be the Easter event. For this event signifies to me that *nothing can separate me from the love of God.* I firmly believe that no sin any of us could commit, or even conceive of committing, is more powerful than God's loving ability to forgive. To believe otherwise, for me, would be to limit God's capacity to love. The Easter event provides the basis for a kind of **hope** and **trust** in a God of love who will abandon me neither in life nor in death. This is reflected in the life, death and resurrection of Jesus, who not only gave us a vision of the character of God but a clear idea of how to live life more meaningfully.

This hope, this trust, in turn, allows me a sense of freedom (as well as responsibility) to strive to be all that I can possibly be within the limitations of my human condition, to strive to seek out and to use those talents and abilities that I might possess.

At the same time, this freedom calls me to think for myself about what it means to be a Christian in the contemporary world with its many uncertainties and ambiguities. It includes the freedom to doubt, to question, to venture out beyond the realm of normally accepted religious dogmas and doctrine, if necessary, for the sake of personal, intellectual and spiritual integrity—as well as for relevance in a ministry with people experiencing the ups and downs of the human condition.

This trust in God, who, I believe, has limited the

range of divine activity by giving us a great deal of freedom to choose the directions we take in life, allows me the freedom to explore all throughout my life the nature of my own personal relationship to God. It frees me to seek God (and truth) wherever I can find God without necessarily restricting myself to those places where others think I ought to look.

This faith, this trust in God, allows me the freedom to recognize that I do not, and will not, need to have all the religious or theological answers to life's many and complex questions. I see that my faith in God is often more of an attitude toward life and its experiences than an answer. It means that I don't have to pretend to be something or someone that I am not. I don't have to try to project a certain kind of religious or pious image.

Therefore, I can feel free to continue to expand my understanding of God's presence in my life and to grow through exploring possible answers to any questions that arise. I thus see the human as a being who is always *potential possibility* as well as present reality. The human is always "on the way," always becoming, never final. I see life as a journey rather than a destination. This in itself is a foundation for hope: With God's help, I have the potential for growth in life. I can feel free to be open to and to experiment with new ideas, concepts and interpretations of life, of God, of the nature of the human condition, of the nature and work of Jesus, of Scripture, and of ministry without feeling threatened, realizing that all such ideas, concepts, doctrines and even biblical interpretations, are humanly created and depend on different perspectives from a myriad of experiences. This awareness, in turn, leads to a certain humility or tentativeness in my own theology, allowing me to be open to new, more meaningful and relevant possibilities in understanding God, life, the world around me and ministering to others.

My trust in this loving, forgiving, compassionate God, who knows something about the limitations and potential of being God-created, gives me the freedom to recognize that I am far from perfect. I am aware of being a very human person who possesses weaknesses as well as strengths, who experiences successes as well as failures, hopes as well as anxieties and fears.

This trust further allows me to admit my own emotions and feelings, whether anger or joy, sadness or fear or jealousy, realizing that only when I admit them to myself can I begin to do something constructive and redemptive with them. As these emotions are redeemed, they begin to contribute to the work of love. I thus minister out of my own flawed, horribly imperfect humanity, not out of some kind of superhuman spiritual superiority, not out of an air of moral perfection, not because I have arrived at some point of religious attainment while other poor souls are still struggling! As a matter of fact, I would suggest that it is *only* when I admit my own humanness that I am truly able to effectively and empathetically minister to others. And when I realize that this "human" ministry is touched by the love of God, I am brought back again to the Easter event.

A More Hopeful Perspective

I enjoy reading through the *Upper Room* series of devotional booklets when I get the chance, looking for different perspectives on what it means to be a person in relationship to God. Three observations from that publication stand out in my mind. Mark Shedron of Colorado observed: "Rather than condemning us for our mistakes God uses them to teach us."[7] George Roberson of North Carolina reflected: "In spite of our peculiarities and bad habits, God sees in us the persons we are created to be."[8] And Mary Kimpston of Iowa said: "God knows about our imperfections and problems but looks at our possibilities, our potential .... God sees our imperfections as possibilities for growth."[9] I find these kinds of statements hopeful and uplifting.

However, all too often, I'm afraid we hear just the opposite, things like:

"God punishes us (or will punish us) for our mistakes in life!"

"God condemns us for our human peculiarities and bad habits!"

"If we are 'good Christians,' we will not have imperfections and problems!"

"God judges us harshly by our past mistakes, *not* by our possibilities and potential!"

"God sees our imperfections as signs of personal weakness or lack of faith!"

Such perspectives on our relationship to God are, to say the least, negative, disheartening, guilt-producing, and often cause despair. They conjure up images that can frighten (I do not believe that we can be frightened into loving God or our fellow humans), that can cause guilt and shame, that can crush the human spirit. These kinds of admonitions (threats?) can make us feel like failures, inadequate to the task of being human: "Why try?" Life can be, and often is, burdensome enough without having to carry the weight of such images and admonitions!

On the other hand, I personally find that the perspectives reflected in the *Upper Room* quotes to be hopeful, encouraging statements about our relationship with God. They say "In spite of all of my past misadventures, bad habits, peculiarities, imperfections and mistakes, there is hope for me! God loves me anyway!" Perhaps, even more radically, "God loves me not in spite of my humanity (with all of its flaws), but because of my humanity!" Such perspectives provide hope, provide encouragement and a kind of energy for the task of living, provide a sense of possibility and potential that we can work toward as we journey through life.

Let's face it, for many if not most of us, as we look back over the trails in our lives, we are painfully aware of the debris and wreckage scattered along the way. We can remember things we have said or done that we should not have. We can remember things that we *should* have said or done that we neglected to do, and we feel guilt and shame. Whether they occurred yesterday or years ago, these memories can be crushing to our sense of self-worth and to our will to go on with life. As we struggle with these memories, the kind of attitude and perspective reflected in these devotional booklets can be refreshing, uplifting and hope-filled.

Further, in these perspectives God is not seen as some kind of cruel, heavy-handed cosmic judge, ready and eager to punish us at our slightest mistake or imperfection (or, worse yet, inflicting some kind of imperfection as a punishment for some sin we have committed). Instead, God is seen as the loving, understanding cosmic encourager and enabler, a Creator who understands the humanness of that Creator's handiwork. That is, we encounter a God who "sees in us the persons we are created to be."

I would risk suggesting that God wants us to use our awareness of our humanness (for peculiarities, problems, bad habits, imperfections and mistakes are a part of what it means to be human) to encourage growth; for our humanness can lead us to develop growing empathy and understanding, patience and appreciation, tolerance and concern and sensitivity toward others (who also struggle with their humanness)—as well as to develop an openness to learning and a willingness to change our ideas of what it means to be human in relationship to God!

The Sacredness of Place

> Then (the Lord) said, "Come no closer! Remove the sandals from your feet, for the place on which you are standing is holy ground."
>
> —Exodus 3: 5

As he reflected on that biblical text, four personal experiences, indelibly etched in his mind, surfaced.

He was an infantry lieutenant at Fort Benning, Georgia, at the time, and on this Saturday morning he and a friend were out attempting to locate a place marked "Ruins" on local topographical maps. The ruins site was on a gentle rise overlooking a shallow, clear creek. Nothing remained of any kind of structure in the area. It had all disappeared—along with its inhabitants—many, many years before. He and his friend from New Jersey poked around in the loose soil and began to find bits and pieces of blue and gray crockery. Someone *had* lived here! As he continued to search for . . . for whatever, he began to be aware of the warm morning sun streaming through the Georgia pines lighting a place of long ago as if to accentuate the sacredness of the place. Real people, real flesh-and-blood people, had once lived here; people who had attempted to scratch out a living here in the Georgia woods, people who had experienced laughter and tears, joy and sorrow, hope and discouragement. He began to imagine an executive in New York City or a movie producer in California or a university professor in Maine or a doctor in Nebraska whose lineage threads through this place.

Come no closer! Remove the sandals from your feet,
for the place on which you are standing is holy ground.

Years later, and miles away, he sat in the warm sand of a dry eastern Colorado creekbed with a local farmer and a professional bone hunter. Cottonwoods shaded them from the summer sun. Recently, an ancient arrowhead had been discovered there by boys playing in the creek, and the experts from back east were there to dig and scrape and brush to see if perhaps more evidence of Paleo-Indians could be found. The three men began to wonder (and to mentally wander) aloud about what life must have been like back then – 10,000-15,000 years ago—on the eastern plains of Colorado. How did those people understand life? How was life made meaningful for them? What made them laugh or cry? How did they deal with birth, with life's twists and turns, with death? What kinds of God or gods and spirits did they believe in, fear, pray to?

Come no closer! Remove the sandals from your feet,
for the place on which you are standing is holy ground.

Once, while visiting his family in Texas, he, along with other family members, went to clean up the cemetery plots of his mother's people in a small rural cemetery near the town of Rowena. When they had finished, he drifted around the cemetery, reading the names and dates etched in stone. At one point, he noticed a couple of small metal markers (the kind mortuaries place as temporary markers until the permanent tombstone arrives) in one weed-infested corner of the cemetery. He walked over and pulled up some of the weeds. It was the grave of an infant. Who was this person? Where was the mother? How must she have felt as she walked away from that tiny grave beneath that vast expanse of Texas sky? Or, perhaps she did not even know where her baby was buried! Did *anyone* know this child? Where were the child's relatives? Dallas? Lubbock? Oklahoma City? Did they ever wonder about her? What is life all about that a child—an infant—is buried in the unkept, weedy corner of a small country cemetery with only a temporary metal marker to indicate the location—to indicate that, for a painfully short while at least, here was a human being?

Come no closer! Remove the sandals from your feet,
for the place on which you are standing is holy ground.

The place was a pediatric intensive care unit in a large Midwestern medical center. The much-too-young-and-innocent mother and father sat across from each other in large wooden rocking chairs, the kind of rocking chairs in which anxiously excited mothers, for the first time, nurse their newborns, while proud but dazed fathers look on. Each took turns holding and rocking and loving their dying infant. He, the pediatric chaplain, stood behind one of the chairs, feeling awkward, feeling sad, feeling the depth of the moment, feeling . . . .

Come no closer! Remove the sandals from your feet,
for the place on which you are standing is holy ground.

A Journey to Last Chance

Some time ago, I came across a church bulletin that had a picture of what appeared to be a vacant farmhouse on the cover. It was bleached-out gray with a gray-white chimney that stood out against a cloudless blue sky. A barbwire fence with a patch of brilliant red flowers (perhaps from an old flower bed once lovingly tended in order to add a splash of beauty to the monotony of the plains) stood in front of the house. That picture reminded me of another house that was the center of some reflections I wrote down after a short trip I once took to Colorado's eastern plains. It was a short trip geographically, but a very long and significant journey spiritually:

> There is something about the wide-open spaces of the plains, an intangible, indescribable something which has much greater attraction to me than the mountains. There is no denying that the mountains are beautiful; there *is* much room to question whether or not the plains could be considered "beautiful," except perhaps in a very intangible way. Perhaps the beauty of the plains lies, at least in part, not in what is there but in what is not there: noise, crowds, pollution, buildings, concrete, asphalt, a limited view. The silence of the plains forces a person to think and to listen inwardly. One is not distracted by the sounds of radios, TVs, cars, airplanes, sirens, construction, other people. In this almost deafening silence, the words of the Psalmist take on a great meaning: "Be still, and know that I am God." Going from the noises

of the city to the silence of the plains reminds me of times past when, after four to six hours on our John Deere tractor, I reached the house at the end of the day, turned off the tractor and immediately became aware of the overwhelming inrush of silence that would fill the void left when the engine stopped running. It is in this silence, this stillness, combined with the "emptiness" which characterizes the plains landscape, that a person is drawn to deep introspection. One feels naked, alone, almost insignificant. There is no hiding from oneself, from one's deeper thoughts, from God.

To get to Last Chance, one must go through such towns as Deer Trail, Agate and River Bend. One crosses Kiowa Creek and Bijou Creek and, if one comes in from the south on Highway 71, one will cross the east fork of Plum Bush Creek. Most of these creeks, very wide and very shallow, run only in season when the winter snows melt. With few exceptions, these creeks are the only areas of the terrain with trees; elsewhere, there are only short grasses and some scrub brush or isolated cactus. Tumbleweeds: One does not see them growing anywhere; but east-west fences which crisscross the otherwise monotonous landscape seem to be collection points for those tumbling from north to south in what is apparently an eternal search for their destination. Lest one wrongly believe that the plains are table-flat, it should be pointed out that, at least in eastern Colorado, there are gently rolling low hills interspersed with those wide, shallow creeks, and there are sudden ravines which are literally invisible until one is on the very edge. Upon seeing one of these phenomena, one begins to appreciate the stories of how large bands of Indians could disappear as they were pursued by cavalry.

Yesterday is mingled with today in the plains. Next to Interstate 70, alone on a small hill, there stands an empty two-story house, a T-shaped house with a large front porch extending the length of the front. One might feel repulsion or sadness at the sight because it is a "dead" house, a reminder of our mortality. One might feel it should be destroyed, for it mars the landscape; such reminders of death should be removed from sight. Yet, that dead house was once very much alive. One can easily imagine the laughter around the house and the shouts of the young couple as they welcomed in the new year, the cries of an infant in the springtime, children playing their summertime games of horseshoes, mud pies and hide-and-seek. It's easy to visualize the house as each of the children grew older and went off to school each autumn, that it felt a sort of inner sense of accomplishment as it listened to the joyous sounds of Christmas coming from the children and grandchildren as they came to visit grandpa and grandma. It is silent now, but perhaps somewhere there is someone who can still remember making those mud pies in the shade it provided on a hot summer day, someone who sees that house not as being dead but as representing a large part of a lifetime. "Shh! Was the noise I just heard that old tumbleweed brushing up against the back porch, or was it the sound of laughter coming from inside?"

As I drove along Highway 71 between Limon and Last Chance, I noticed a crumbling adobe building standing in one of those treeless pastures just to the east of the road. I stopped to take a picture of it. Immediately upon getting out of the car I noticed that all was silent except

> for a single meadowlark perched on one of the remaining rafters of the building. His shrill call pierced the stillness; it was, for a brief moment in eternity, a sermon in song about Life. In that stillness, my soul was cleared of all pollution and dirt. I felt suddenly clean.

Can we see the presence of God in the seemingly ordinary, or hear the presence of God in the commonplace, or feel the presence of God in the everyday routine?

Can we draw spiritual nourishment from the vast emptiness of the eastern Colorado plains as well as from a full church, from dry creekbeds cluttered with last fall's leaves as well as from stained glass windows in a massive cathedral, from the music of a solitary meadowlark as well as from the voices of a great choir, from the deafening silence of an abandoned prairie home as well as from the silent prayer in a worship service?

Memorial Day: A Different Perspective

May—the month when we observe Memorial Day, and when millions of kids celebrate the end of another school year.

I grew up on a farm in west Texas, and the best I can remember, Memorial Day was completely overshadowed by the end of school! I don't remember any particular ceremonies or special events which marked that day. The first time I really became aware of Memorial Day as a significant event was when I was pastoring a small rural church in deep eastern Colorado. For those people, it was better known as Decoration Day, a time when one paused to remember not only military veterans but all of those significant persons who were no longer living.

On the Sunday before Memorial Day, Sunday School teachers would take their students across the gravel road to the church cemetery to read the names and dates on the stones. After church, many of the adults would walk across the road, talking in hushed tones (perhaps as a sign of respect—or not to disturb the dead?) about people of other times and places. Or the men would talk about the possibility of a bumper wheat crop coming in July (perhaps so as not to touch within themselves feelings so deep they might bring forth a tear or a choked voice). There would be grave markers among the cedars (representing eternal life) aged by the years of summer rain and winter blizzards. There were other markers where the turned earth was as fresh as the sadness and grief.

All that next day, Memorial Day, in the late-May warmth, to the singing of meadowlarks on nearby fence posts, people in Chevrolets and Fords would pull off into the shallow, freshly mowed ditch, walk over to certain gray-white stones, place a handful of flowers on the ground and then stand silently looking out across the great expanse of cultivated prairie. Perhaps they were looking into the past, struggling to remember what Uncle Ed looked like in his World War I uniform, or how Aunt Annie sounded as she sang in the church choir. There were other graves, too, the graves of children; lives cut short by the flu epidemic of the early years of the century.

Memorial Day: a time when we struggle in mostly inadequate ways to say, "Thank you"... "I loved you" to people we usually failed to say such things to when they were alive. A time when we attempt to appreciate the trials and hardships, the hopes and dreams, the victories and defeats of those who are no longer with us (as we hope others will appreciate what *we* have gone through). A day when we make the effort to forgive someone whom we feel wronged us, or to ask for forgiveness of those we feel we have wronged. It is an effort at a kind of immortality ("As long as we can remember Aunt June, she will not really be gone.").

Memorial Day: a day when we pause from our routines to remember those who have made us who we are, those whose lives have touched ours in some meaningful way, and whose lives were touched by ours.

What Is Really Important? (I)

With what shall I come before the Lord, and bow myself before God on high? Shall I come before Him with burnt offerings, with calves a year old? Will the Lord be pleased with thousands of rams, with ten thousands of rivers of oil? Shall I give my firstborn for my transgression, the fruit of my body for the sin of my soul? He has told you, O mortal, what is good; and what does the Lord require of you but to do justice, and to love kindness, and to walk humbly with your God?

–Micah 6: 6-8

Woe to you, scribes and Pharisees, hypocrites! For you tithe mint, dill, and cumin, and have neglected the weightier matters of the law: justice and mercy and faith. It is these you ought to have practiced without neglecting the others. You blind guides! You strain out a gnat but swallow a camel!

–Matthew 23: 23-24

If I speak in the tongues of mortals and of angels but do not have love, I am a noisy gong or a clanging symbol. And if I have prophetic powers, and understand all mysteries and all knowledge, and if I have all faith, so as to remove mountains, but do not have love, I am nothing. If I give away all my possessions, and if I hand over my body so that I may boast, but do not have love, I gain nothing.

–I Corinthians 13: 1-3

While religious activities and talents, and biblical knowledge are important, they cannot be a substitute for loving our fellow human beings: "For the whole law is summed up in a single commandment, 'You shall love your neighbor as yourself'" (Galatians 5: 14). I personally believe that this is the heart and soul of the Christian life.

All too often, many people I encounter tend to describe or define the "real," devout Christian in terms of a person who seems extremely knowledgeable about the Bible, the person who seems to always have a definite, unchallengeable understanding of what each Scripture text or story means, the person who has supposedly read the Bible from cover to cover at least once, the person who attends church two or three or four times a week, the person who is certain that she/he knows the very day the world will come to an end, the person who seems (on the surface, at least) to have life all put together with no worries or problems, the person who sprinkles his/her normal, everyday conversations with numerous religious words and phrases.

Tragically, I seldom hear anyone speak of a person being a real, devout Christian in terms of being very loving, caring, understanding, compassionate, accessible and patient. By contrast, rarely would someone feel free to turn to "religious" persons because they tend to be morally self-righteous and spiritually smug, as well as being preachy with simplistic, pat answers, especially to *others'* problems! Also, since they seem to have the puzzle of life all put together, they don't seem to be able to appreciate the struggles of more common folk who are still attempting to find all the pieces. (Perhaps some feel that these kinds of Christians must be protected from the reality of the human condition!) Quite simply, a loving attitude does not seem to be part of the popular image or definition of what being a Christian is all about. And that's sad.

But let's face it: Loving others is terribly difficult to do! It is much, much easier (and safer) to make Christianity a religion of religious activities and religious knowledge than it is to make it a spiritual lifestyle based on loving others. Gorden Poteat, commenting on the New Testament book of James, expressed the dilemma this way:

> James . . . follows his predecessors . . . in conceiving of man's relationship to God as dependent upon . . . a simple and sincere devotion to God, demonstrated by compassionate relationship with one's fellows . . . . Such an understanding of religion is so simple that many have been unable to believe it to be adequate. But it is so difficult to practice that ceremonies with the most complicated elaboration have been found easier to offer God in its stead.[10]

To which I would add: not only "ceremonies with the most complicated elaboration," but also things like church attendance and biblical and theological knowledge are "found easier to offer to God in its stead!"

Further, I would risk suggesting that love is an attitude (a way of seeing things, a way of relating) not only toward ourselves (for unless we can love ourselves, we cannot expend the energy necessary in loving others) and other people, but also toward the natural nonhuman world in which we live and survive. Such a larger sense of loving others involves, among other things, a sense of the importance and significance of the other. The other is not an object to be used, abused, manipulated and deceived for our own personal benefit, advancement or welfare. Love means having an appreciation for the other's struggles and the other's story. It is an ongoing attempt to understand what the other is experiencing. (I use the phrase ongoing attempt because I don't believe that any person is perfectly loving: it is a lifelong process of trial and error.) Loving others means, among other things, developing what I call redemptive, existential empathy, that is, a kind of understanding and appreciation of what it means to be human (or a creature of God). This happens through a process of honestly reflecting upon one's own life experiences, especially the more painful ones, and an ongoing attempt to understand the life-struggles of others. Such empathy leads to a sense of connectedness to other human beings and a desire to make life a little more livable for us all. Loving others requires more an attitude of sharing and cooperation than competition. Loving calls for becoming as much other-centered as self-centered.

In the end, only love works. While hate, war, abuse, lying, prejudice, cheating, selfishness, manipulation of others, intolerance and arrogance (including religious intolerance and arrogance), vindictiveness, bigotry—to name just a few—may seem to work in the short run; in the long run these attitudes are ultimately destructive. They are corrosive of the human spirit. They are a kind of spiritual cancer that tears away at our very being, at our ability to be fully human, making us less than God wants us to be. In the end, only love works.

What Is Really Important? (II)

In the last reflection I suggested that the attitude of love is not limited to oneself and to others, but is also to be shown "toward the natural nonhuman world in which we live and survive." I suspect that as we transition into the twenty-first century we are becoming painfully aware of the need to love and care for the nonhuman part of the natural world. More and more we are realizing that we are very much a part of it, not *apart* from it!

Tragically, throughout the history of the Christian Church, we all too often have understood biblical texts such as Genesis 1: 26, ". . . 'Let us make humankind in our image . . . and let them have dominion . . . over all the wild animals of the earth, and over every creeping thing that creeps upon the earth,'" and Psalm 8, "You have given them dominion over the works of your hands; you have put all things under their feet," to mean that it is our God-given right to run roughshod over nature for our own enjoyment and benefit. We have believed that nature, in the form of wildlife, plantlife, minerals, water, etc., has been given to us "superior" humans by God to use as we please. Further, people have assumed that God would provide an endless supply of nature. We have often even thought of the natural world as the enemy of progress, that it has to be conquered or tamed, most often by destruction.

For example, when I was growing up in the farm and ranch country of West Texas, our immediate (unthinking and unquestioning) response to the presence of wildlife was to hurriedly get a rifle and shoot. Wild animals and various kinds of birds were considered pests, varmints, predators. No one that I know of ever considered the possibility that their presence might do more good than harm—or at least did not do as much harm as we claimed. Perhaps no one *wanted* to think that way: It was too much fun shooting them. It made us feel in control, all-powerful (or at least more powerful than the animal we had just killed), perhaps even godlike. And I cannot remember anyone ever suggesting that we use live-animal traps to transfer them to a more appropriate area.

I once came across an article by Peter Singer about a political controversy over the damming of a river in a remote part of Australia. It proposed a very different perspective of the relationship between humans and nonhuman nature:

> Perhaps the best that can be said about the preservation of wilderness—apart from the value of the wilderness for the sentient creatures that live in it or will pass through it—is that respect for wilderness is a sign of much needed humility on the part of our species. When we clear the bush, dam the rivers and push freeways across the countryside, we're thinking of ourselves and our mastery of nature. When we stop doing these things we can appreciate the complex living world that existed long before we did and still gets along very nicely without us. Only then can we see ourselves in perspective, not as the source of everything that is of value, but as beings who exist alongside a myriad of different forms of life, and do not possess any inherent right to dominion over them.[11]

In this light, perhaps a part of loving nature is to

become more and more aware of our relationship to it, to see human life as inextricably intertwined with it, to realize that God also created it (and, thus, that it has value in and of itself, regardless of our presence or absence). Perhaps loving the natural nonhuman world begins by attempting to learn about it—and not just so that we can exploit it. We can learn to respect it for its power (as in respecting the power of a rattlesnake!) but also to appreciate it for its own sake. Perhaps we can love the natural world around us by learning to see the sacred in the seemingly ordinary. We can find creative alternatives to death and destruction when we are at odds with nature. We can restructure and reframe our values, our goals, our priorities and lifestyles so they become less destructive of the natural world. Perhaps such an attitude of loving the natural world may help us appreciate how being (what kind of person we are) rather than having (how much money, power, material possessions we can accumulate) is a true measurement of success and of what is really important in life.

Some Thoughts in the Middle of the Year

> No person lives under ideal circumstances. Life is offered to each individual on different terms. Life comes to mean somewhat different things to different persons. Yet, each human being can seek such fulfillment as is possible and appropriate to his situation. It is not a matter of having everything or nothing. Life is the art of the possible. To seek the possibilities in each situation for sensitive, appreciative, creative living is to seek the way of life fulfillment and celebration.[12]
>
> —Harvey Potthoff, *God and the Celebration of Life*

Near the halfway mark of this year, and into my birthday month of July, I am aware of *time's arrow*, aware that each of us is on a kind of journey, a journey through space and time. This journey through space includes the various geographical locations we have lived in and travelled to and their impact upon how we see and understand life. The journey through time reflects the historical era we live in as well as our chronological age at any particular point along the way. I often envision the human saga as a caravan moving through history that we as individuals join at some point—and then, sooner or later, leave. In this human journey—this caravan—we are all travelling from somewhere, and, by and large, each of our journeys to this point has been unique, each of our life stories different. We are born into and grow up in a great variety of circumstances, not all of them positive, not all of them conducive to growth and life. For some, in the words of Loren Eiseley, life seems like a "long crucifixion."[13] For others, it is a series of challenging, growth-producing opportunities. The longer I am in the business of pastoral care and have the opportunity to listen to the life stories of many and varied individuals, the more I can appreciate Potthoff's comment that life "is offered to each individual on different terms." We, therefore, bring to the present moment not only our biologically inherited traits and characteristics, but also the results of the many experiences, good and bad, personal victories and defeats, failures and successes, personal experiences with loss, grief, joy and celebration, good times and not-so-good times, wrong decisions and right choices. Because each of our space-time journeys has been different, because "life is offered to each individual on different terms," I find that we bring very different perspectives into conversations with one another. Perhaps Loren Eiseley had a point when he observed: "But men see differently. I can at best report only from my own wilderness."[14]

Thus, to make our story normative, a measure by which all others are judged, is to close one's mind to the richness and diversity that is a part of this human caravan. We need to continue to work on *listening* to the stories—the experiences—of others, not so that we might condemn or belittle or even approve of others but that we might appreciate them for who they are and for what they have been through and are going through. As we would have others listen to us and appreciate the importance that our life-story has for us, so we also can be appreciative of their stories. We can help each other "seek such fulfillment as is possible and appropriate to his situation" through listening, not only to the words but also to the feelings behind and underneath the words. Perhaps, in the process, we shall become even more appreciative of the life around us—and life as "the art of the possible."

Too Much of a Good Thing?

> What had I gained from all my inspirational reading if I didn't practice it?[15]
>
> –Sue Lennon

Some time ago, as I was catching up on my Bible reading, I began to realize that I could spend all of my time reading and never be out among people—and that, ironically, the more of the Bible I read, the less ministering among others I would do! I was reminded that there has to be a kind of balance between inspirational reading and involvement among people, between action and reflection.

At the same time I realized that reading inspirational literature or the Bible or books on theology can be a way to feel religious while deliberately avoiding dealing with people in their everyday affairs! Let's face it, it is much easier, simpler, safer and cleaner to be a Christian if being a Christian is defined by things like frequently reading the Bible and devotional literature, attending many church-related activities and attempting to act pious (that is, without serious sin or moral blemish and sprinkling one's daily conversations with a large dose of religious language, etc.) It is much, much easier than if being a Christian calls for us to struggle to relate to and to empathize with people in their personal needs and hurts, needs and hurts that often seem beyond our ability to fix with simple answers!

Unfortunately, when it comes to living the Christian life, many of us can very readily relate to Charlie Brown –or was it Linus?–who shouted: "I love humanity! It's people I can't stand!" That is, we would rather simply talk about loving humanity as a broad, abstract category—or feel loving—than to practice loving the individual, unique people we have to put up with every day. To deal with real, particular people in everyday nitty-gritty situations is too messy. It muddies the otherwise crystal-clear waters of our simplistic, comfortable, pat religious answers; nor can we always be in control of the situation! There is a temptation to hide behind our Bible or inspirational reading rather than be disturbed and interrupted by the life-concerns of stumbling, bumbling, sinful—and irritating—human beings. They are so unpredictable and ungrateful! So we really limit ourselves to talking about all of those wonderful Bible stories and their larger-than-life characters, and about how much we love Jesus and how wonderful and loving Jesus is to us, rather than listening to and becoming involved in the hopes and fears and struggles of others.

Because of this, we tend to separate our Christian life from the rest of life, to compartmentalize our life into the religious or sacred and the secular. And we hope that God judges us by our religious life, *not* by our secular everyday life. We hope God will see our Sunday-morning-go-to-meeting smiles, *not* how we relate to other drivers during weekday traffic jams. We hope our Christianity will be defined by how many Bible verses we have memorized or the number of Sunday School attendance pins we have accumulated, *not* by how we have handled those many occasions when cheating or deception would give us the advantage or ensure personal gain.

Of course, reading the Bible can be a great foundation and a great aid to living a truly Christian life, but we need to be careful that our inspirational reading remains a means to an end, not an end in itself (not a way of chalking up merits with God!). It should be a way of better understanding how God works in our lives and through our lives, renewing hope within us during those times when things don't seem hopeful, a way of better understanding and appreciating and becoming more sensitive to the human lives we encounter each day. If we hold to these attitudes, not only will our spiritual reading help us make life a little more livable for others—and, consequently, for ourselves—we also won't be getting *too much of a good thing*!

On Doing the Lord's Work

"Oh, Chaplain, are you out doing the Lord's work this morning?"

I must admit that every time I hear something like this, I feel very uncomfortable. Just what does it mean "to do the Lord's work"?

In this, I am reminded of an encounter with a retiring nurse many years ago in Wichita, Kansas. She excitedly came up to me in the hallway and announced that she was retiring after many years of nursing, and that now she would go to "work for the Lord." In my usual inappropriate way, I started to suggest to her that perhaps all of those years of working with and caring for hospital patients could be seen as working for the Lord. However, she curtly cut me off, saying, "Don't give me that!" As she resisted equating being a nurse with doing the Lord's work, she was doing what many people do: separating our Christian life from the rest of life.

Her image of doing the Lord's work probably included such church-centered activities as preaching, Sunday School teaching, working with church youth groups, women's guild, covered-dish suppers, church cleanups, giving to missions, seasonal church decorating and sending cards to shut-ins and to ill members of a congregation. Such activities are good and valuable; they are also relatively safe, organized, structured, comfortably familiar, and controlled. On the other hand, nursing is often neither safe nor organized and structured.

Many times one is very much not in control of a

situation. In health care, one deals with a lot of physically and psycho-spiritually hurting people, people who can at times be anxious and fearful, angry, uncooperative and unappreciative. (I've been a hospital patient!) In other words, it involves people and situations that can draw the worst out of a caregiver if he or she is not careful—people and situations that can try one's patience, sympathy, good intentions, kindness. Caregiving provides experiences that can force you to look into an existential mirror to see the "real you," and that image can be very disturbing. It's hard to show Christian love, patience, understanding, forgiveness, forbearance and compassion toward those people and in those situations that make us see our "bad" side. Perhaps such thoughts and memories raced through that nurses's mind when I started to suggest that nursing could be understood as doing the Lord's work, and the thoughts were unsettling.

I personally believe that doing the Lord's work (and there is a case to be made that the Lord has done—and is doing—"the Lord's work." *Our* task is to do *our* work!) has a great deal to do with human relationships. Anytime there are people loving and caring for other people—be they nurses compassionately working among the ill or even, God forbid, politicians struggling to come up with legislation that gives all people equal opportunities, making our society a better place in which to live for all its members—I suspect that God is there. That is, the Lord is with us "doing the Lord's work." I would risk going so far as to suggest that even when a person does not think that he/she is doing the Lord's work, if that person is making life a little more livable for others, if that person is consciously struggling to have an attitude of love, compassion and redemptive existential empathy (that is, an appreciation of what it means to be human, an appreciation then translated into a contributive lifestyle), that person is, in fact, "doing the Lord's work!"

Windmill Memories: A Spiritual Journey

Each journey—each return—to southwest Texas to visit my family has been a spiritual journey, a journey back to the foundations of my personal story. I grew up on an expanse of farmland called, with reason, Lipan Flats by the locals. Looking east on a clear day, one can almost see the birth of tomorrow; looking west, one can faintly make out the last minutes of yesterday. On a clear night, the Milky Way bands across the ink-black sky from horizon to horizon.

That land is so open that one can watch rain showers travelling across the nearby cotton and milo farms, watch with the hope that their journey will take them over one's own farm.

Then, of course, there is the sound of rain on the tin roof. (The last words my father spoke to me when our hoeing goatheads was interrupted by a summer shower, a few minutes before he died of a heart attack in July, 1961, were that he was "going into the barn to watch it rain," where he could also hear the rain on the barn's tin roof).

Prominent on the flatland terrain, windmills were an integral part of every farm. The image of the windmill was so powerful for me that years later, in an effort to capture some of the memories of my childhood, I would write:

> The weeds and wild grasses have grown up around it now that it stands alone, unused. The wooden tower, once rich in color, has turned a grayish brown from its exposure to the natural elements. Rust streaks down from the nails. Time has taken its toll on some of the cross-beams, split and hanging limply.
>
> It is a monument to another time—a mute testimony to a life that was.
>
> There was a time when the whirring of the wheel and the clunking of the rods were familiar daily sounds—sounds that became part of one's self, part of one's soul—sounds that put one to sleep on gentle moonlit summer nights. They were reassuring sounds that lulled one to sleep with the feeling that all was right with life, that tomorrow would bring forth new life, new adventures. They were sounds that alerted one to changing winds in the path of an oncoming thunderstorm. At the end of the day when the only sound from living creatures was the thrill call of the mockingbird, one could still hear the familiar sound of the windmill adding a securing constancy to life.
>
> Now it stands alone, silent, unused, unneeded, slowly, surely giving way to the actions of time.
>
> But somewhere, in distant places, there are those who remember it in moments of quiet, who remember the peace of mind—the peace of soul—it provided, who remember an innocent time of childhood, and they quietly gaze into the distance and smile to themselves.

Such vivid memories etch the pattern of my life story—my personal, unique life story. But then, I am aware that we *all* have (or, perhaps more accurately, *are*) our own individual life stories, stories intertwined with the unique life stories of many others. Our stories give us a sense of who we are, a sense of connectedness and belonging, an understanding of where we have come from, even an appreciation of why we are the way we are. Genealogies, family trees, and reunions are attempts to reconstruct and connect our stories. The ancient Hebrews seemed very much aware of the importance of story:

> When your children ask you in the time to come, "What is the meaning of the decrees and the statutes and the ordinances that the Lord our God has commanded you?" then you shall say to your children, "We were Pharaoh's slaves in Egypt, but the Lord brought us out of Egypt with a mighty hand . . ." (Deuteronomy 6: 20-23).

Perhaps it is not going too far to suggest that our reactions to and interpretations of life's daily experiences, our perceptions of reality, and our opinions about life are born of our personal stories. I would even suggest that how we understand and interpret the Bible and other sacred writings (and the preacher on Sunday morning) is shaped by our own story. Several years ago, as I was paying for a meal at a Missouri restaurant, the cashier asked, "Where are you travelling *from?*" The way she worded the question intrigued me, and all the way back home that day I reflected on her question as it applied to my life journey. We are all travelling *from* somewhere. We don't come to our todays out of a vacuum: We bring to each day all of our yesterdays, for good or ill. We are all coming from somewhere (places, life-experiences, historical eras, etc.) and those somewheres affect our todays and tomorrows. As Wendy M. Wright observed in a *Weavings* article entitled "Memories of Now":

> My past shapes my present, but my present remembering also shapes my past. How I claim it—graciously, with forgiveness and gratitude, or not so graciously, with bitter nostalgia or remorse—is important. All these memories have given the present moment the shape it has now. They are the stuff of God-with-me, the places, times, and events once present tense that have changed, challenged, and invited me to experience the simple truth that God meets me here. Not where I think I ought to be. Nor where I once was. Nor where I might some day be. But in my story. Here. As I am. Now.[16]

Spiritual Variations on the Theme of Railroads

Several years ago when I was visiting my mother near San Angelo, Texas, I decided to drive by the old railroad roundhouse that had been an important landmark in my early years. It was going to be one of those personal spiritual journeys to reconnect with a part of my past in order to provide a kind of reassuring security to my present. Dark, greasy, glorious, the roundhouse and its turntable had been the site of field trips when I was in grade school. To ride around on the turntable ("Now don't get your toes caught in the gears!") and to walk around inside that cavernous building among those awesome steam locomotives ("Now don't lean up against that engine or you'll get grease on you!") had been a frighteningly exhilarating experience! On occasion, my Dad would drive there so I could look, but to my way of thinking he would get too close to those black behemoths. My anxiety would rise as we drew nearer and nearer!

That roundhouse was a part of who I was, of who I am—an integral and foundational part of the landscape of the memories of my life. As I drove to the location of the roundhouse on that sunny morning, hard reality gave me a shock! It was no longer there! In its place were bright, shiny warehouses set on white gravel lots! "How could they have done this to me, to take away a part of who I am?!" All of those years I was away from home I had felt a sense of stability and connectedness—even if most of the landmarks of my past might disappear, at least the old roundhouse would surely always be there, just as it had been in my memories!

Several years later, as my wife and son and I were driving to visit my mother, on the highway between Abilene and Winters, Texas, I began to notice what appeared to be extensive work on the railroad that ran parallel to the highway, a railroad that had obviously been there since the beginning of time and would surely be there throughout eternity. Then it hit me: They're dismantling the railroad! My first impulse was to stop the car and shout at the workers:

> Hey! Wait a minute! You're tearing up my past! You're ripping up part of the foundation of the building of my life! You're dismantling my personal image of reality! You're desecrating the landscape of my life! Please, please give me a few minutes to sit here and absorb what is happening! Give me one last chance to fix in my mind's eye this railroad as I want to remember it!

More recently, I came across over 100 photographic negatives, sixty to eighty years old, that my mother had accumulated in her early years in Concho County, Texas. One of the negatives, in particular, turned out to be a great treasure: the picture of a freight train steaming through a winter day on my grandparents' ranch during the 1920s! In 1909, the first leg of what was to be a railroad that ran down into central Texas was built from Miles to Paint Rock. It went right through my grandparents' ranch. However, due to economic conditions, it was never completed, and was dismantled around 1937. I remember, as I was growing up, roaming through the abandoned right-of-way near my grandparents' house, finding old railroad spikes and the decaying trestle pilings over a shallow creek just to the west of their house. At the time, such things meant very little to me. They would surely always be there if I needed them! However, as we age, such things of the past tend to take on renewed significance, perhaps because more and more of our life is in the past! So, finding that old negative was exciting! The train in the photo was just as my mother had described it: a steam locomotive, a passenger car, box cars and cattle cars. It was like a ghost image out of the past. Those were real people on that train—real flesh-and-blood people who had built that railroad through cotton fields and mesquite pastures. To them, the railroad represented hope. Now it was all gone, and most of the people who had been a part of that railroad were too. (My mother, while looking at the images in those old photos, sighed: ". . . to realize that they are all dead.")

I was very much aware that extremely little physical evidence of that railroad remained. However, I was certain that the pilings of that trestle would still be there. Shortly thereafter, I decided to go back to that place with my older brother (a kind of spiritual pilgrimage) to get some pictures. On one of those hot West Texas summer days, we weaved our way through dense growths of mesquite and prickly pear which had overgrown the right-of-way over the past sixty years to the place where we remembered the trestle to be. Disappointment . . . sudden sadness: All that was there was the eroding grade and the gap where the trestle had spanned the creek—and even it seemed more modest than I remembered it being. There were no signs of pilings. Nothing, not even the large tree we both remembered shading the trestle. Several feet away in the dry creek bed lay one round piling, hollowed by the years. I felt sad: Another part of my past, a past that I had carried in my memories, was no longer there. As I walked away, I felt a deep and quiet sense of loss.

In each of these railroad experiences, my task became one of reorganizing my memories, restructuring my view of reality: To my memories I would now add the realization that the objects of those memories—the roundhouse, the railroad tracks, the trestle pilings—are no longer there. In the process of this restructuring, I would change. I could no longer count on the past always being there for me, providing a comforting, secure sameness. My perception of reality, even the reality of my memories, was subject to constant change, a lesson I would relearn over and over again in life.

Redeeming the Pain of Life

T. H. Watkins, in *The Great Depression*, wrote of Eleanor Roosevelt:

> As the daughter of an alcoholic father and a distant, critical mother—both of whom had died before Eleanor was ten years old—Mrs. Roosevelt had endured an excruciating childhood, nearly empty of both parental contact and emotional stability. Surviving that bleak upbringing could have embittered her; instead, it had nurtured deep-felt concern for the deprived and downtrodden, which not only had complemented the instincts of her husband but had encouraged and enlarged them.[17]

Reading this reminded me, again, that one of the primary characteristics of the Christian life is not so much what happens to us in life as how we react to what happens to us! We cannot always control the things that happen to us or keep them from happening, but we do have some control or influence or choices over how we will react to those experiences—what we will do with them.

An example of this was related to me several years ago by an ex-prisoner of war. When he had returned to the United States after World War II, he was full of vindictiveness and hate toward his former captors for all that they had done to him and his fellow captives. Sometime after he returned, he was asked to talk to a local church group about his POW experience, and that led to other talks to other groups. Gradually, over time, the talks began to have a therapeutic effect. The anger and resentment gently, quietly began to disappear. He was able to overcome the bitterness and hate (if left unchecked, these spiritual cancers can eventually destroy one's humanity) and develop a more redemptive perspective on that horrible, unforgettable experience, a perspective out of which he would be able to contribute to the knowledge and understanding of others.

On another occasion I spoke with a person who had suffered a stroke several years earlier. He told me that as he struggled with his own disability he decided to become involved in a stroke support group. He felt it would not only aid his own recovery but that he also might be able to help others who had just suffered a stroke. He could have decided that for all intents and purposes his life was over—that he no longer had anything to offer life. Instead, he chose to take that experience and do something contributive with it.

An elderly patient, in reviewing his life, once told me how at one point life had become so painful that he seriously contemplated suicide ("Chaplain, I stood on the edge of the abyss, but, at the last minute, I stepped back."). This man easily could have become self-righteously unsympathetic toward those who had also "stood on the edge of the abyss" and decided to step off. Instead, he said: "I can understand those who *do* go over the edge." He had taken his own pain and let it lead him to an understanding and empathy for others who know a similar pain.

In *Twenty-Four Hours a Day*, a publication directed to people in Alcoholics Anonymous, addiction is to be seen not only as a great challenge to overcome, but also as a unique opportunity to help others:

> In A.A. we learn that since we are alcoholics we can be uniquely useful people. That is, we can help other alcoholics when perhaps somebody

> who has not had our experience with drinking could not help them. That makes us uniquely useful. The A.A.s are a unique group of people because they have taken their own greatest defeat and failure and sickness and used it as a means of helping others.[18]

What are we to do with painful experiences of life such as illness, accident, physical disability, divorce, estrangement from family, alcohol or drug addiction, the wounds of war, loss of a job, aging, the death of a loved one, broken relationships, and on and on? We can use painful experiences of the past as excuses or rationalizations for subsequent failures and problems. We can spend the rest of our lives feeling like victims, making a career out of blaming others (or God) for what happened to us many years ago. We can adopt a kind of perverse self-justifying, self-satisfying perspective which makes us feel spiritually or morally superior to others. We can allow our experience to make us bitter, rigidly dogmatic and unbending in our attitude toward the world, unforgiving, cold, unfeeling and even self-righteously vengeful.

I do not believe that Christians are somehow immune to the human condition, that they are somehow protected by God from suffering and defeat and failure. As a matter of fact, instead of believing that they are going to be spared the pain of life, Christians, more than anyone else, ought to be aware that to be human is to be susceptible to suffering. Christians ought thus to be on the forefront of the human endeavor to alleviate as much suffering as possible—and to make inevitable suffering less painful and less destructive to the human spirit, and more redemptive. I would suggest that the Christian should see suffering more as a challenge to be redemptively overcome than as a burden to be borne or an excuse to be used as a crutch. As Eleanor Roosevelt reminds us, Christians ought to be the very persons who proclaim to the world, more through their actions than their words, that the pain of the human condition can be overcome, can be redeemed. For Christians, any suffering can be redeemed, turned into something contributive to the lives of others and, consequently, to their own lives.

The Secret Hurts of Life

Out There . . . In Here

Out there, it's springtime with snow melting and with
robins singing;
In here, it's still winter, cold and bleak.

Out there, they say I have a sense of humor;
In here, humor doesn't exist.

Out there, it is said that I must be a happy person;
In here, there is only a very deep sadness.

Out there, people say that I never take anything seriously;
In here, the seriousness of life weighs heavily upon this
soul.

Out there, some think that I am busy with friends;
In here, the loneliness is overwhelming.

We all have them, those hidden hurts that cut deep within our being but that are too private or personal or intimate to share with others. That secret hurt may be a personal sense of failure at life, loving or being loved. It may be the gnawing feeling that one's life is no longer meaningful or that all of those dreams and visions of one's youth are shattered, scattered across the floor like so many pieces of fragile glass. That secret woundedness may be the grief of the loss of a hoped-for child, stillborn or miscarried; or the loss of a loved one through suicide, an experience so tragically stigmatized by society (and the church) that one is afraid—or too ashamed—to talk about it. It may be the frustrating feeling of being imprisoned or trapped by circumstances, that one has been backed into a corner in life with no way out. That secret hurt may be a burning rage: at life, at fate, at God, for the seeming unfairness or injustice that seems to pervade all of human existence. It may be a horrible emptiness brought on by rejection or abandonment or betrayal by a close friend or loved one, perhaps through divorce. It may be the numbing feelings of guilt and shame brought on by the thought that one has failed a loved one, that one has not measured up (as a spouse or a parent or an employee, or even as a human being), damaging—tearing at—one's self-image and sense of self-worth. Especially among those of us who are wartime veterans, there can be a deep sense of guilt or shame for the things we did or failed to do while in combat, failures which caused injury or death to others—and, consequently, a kind of spiritual death within ourselves.

These are but a few of the secret hurts of life, the kind that can drag us down, eroding our enthusiasm for living, making us wonder if life is worth the effort.

Perhaps we would like to share our pain, to tell someone our story, but are afraid to. We may be ridiculed, or not taken seriously ("If you think your experience was bad, listen to this!"). We're afraid that we may be considered weak, or may be accused of not having enough faith or of making a mountain out of a molehill. We're afraid that others will tell us (out of their own personal discomfort with our pain) that we should "get over it" or "not dwell on it." We are told that "big men don't cry" or that "you shouldn't feel that way." We're afraid that others will think less of us if we acknowledge that we have secret hurts, that others will hold them against us.

As a result, we wear masks, masks that hide the tears, the anger, the loneliness, the deep, deep hurt. Like the author of the poem at the beginning of this reflection, we struggle to continue the journey with those feelings churning within us, and we feel that no one truly cares, that no one truly understands and appreciates the pain we feel. We feel the chill of loneliness in a frighteningly vast and seemingly indifferent universe. Others see only our exterior—the side we present to the public—not the inside, the inner self that bleeds.

Out of these secret hurts, out of our own awareness of the pain we feel, we must strive toward what I call redemptive existential empathy. It's an appreciation of what it means to be human, an appreciation then translated into a compassionate, contributive lifestyle. Somehow, in the midst of and out of our own woundedness, we must work on developing personal trustworthiness, that is, a sense of accessibility, openness and acceptance so that others will feel comfortable sharing their deepest hurts and joys with us. We must struggle to make each other know that we are all truly worth the effort to overcome those secret hurts.

October

October. Autumn. It is a time of year when we are reminded of change, when we are especially aware of "time's arrow," when we most often sense movement in our life journeys. It can be an especially quiet time, a quiet and gentle time. For me personally it tends to be a sad time, a time to look inward and a time to reflect. It's a time to ask: "What's it all about, what's life all about?"

Eugene Kennedy, in *The Joy of Being Human*, wrote of autumn:

> Things are never quite the same after the Labor Day holiday even though it is technically still summer and the days are as warm and appealing as freshly buttered toast. The wind has a sigh in it which says that the days are changing . . . and so are we, right along with them. Autumn tells us, in a way that no other season can, that time is passing; perhaps because of the days' deepening mellowness which somehow says that the year is spending itself all too quickly, we realize that we have not quite caught up with the changing season, or with many of those important things that are always just beyond our grasp in life. The winter may try a man's soul but the fall can break his heart; it is too full of things just ending and others yet to be done, too rich in memory and promise not to turn a person inward for a while.[19]

I suspect that we strive to become involved in all of those various autumn activities—like football, social events and harvesttime festivals—at least in part so that we won't have to touch those deep feelings and "long thoughts" attempting to surface as the year begins to slide toward a close. We avoid the inward turning of autumn so that we won't have to deal with those reflections and memories of times and experiences past and the realization that our life, and the lives of loved ones, like the passing year, are a little nearer to their end.

Autumn. Memories, personal and unique: memories of growling cotton gins and the aroma of burning cotton burrs drifting with a wisp of white smoke across the West Texas farmland of Lipan Flats.

Autumn. Memories and images: a patch of sunlight. When, as I was growing up, our family would visit my grandparents' ranch on one of those "cat-lying-in-the-sun" autumn Sundays, I was often required to take a nap after lunch. My place was on my great uncle's bed in a room chilled by the north wind. I would crawl under one of those heavy homemade quilts, with a patch of that late-year, south-leaning sunlight streaming through the window to warm me to sleep. Except for the movement of a yellowjacket wasp in the high corner of the window seeking out the last life-giving warmth of the year, there was a certain stillness, a certain apartness from the world in that room that penetrated to the depths of my soul. When I would wake up later, I would notice how that patch of sunlight on the quilt had shifted with the afternoon sun: a quiet and gentle reminder of time's arrow.

I believe it's O.K. to have these kinds of "long thoughts" about life. I believe it's O.K. to feel deeply, even to feel a certain sadness from time to time. It means that we are in touch with the human condition, with what it means to be human in all its glory and all its agony. I question whether or not we can truly "rejoice with those who rejoice, weep with those who weep" unless and until we can accept and appreciate our own personal God-given feelings of joy and sorrow. I suspect that the more we are in touch with our own deeper thoughts and feelings, the more compassionate and understanding, the more forgiving and patient we will be of others—the more we will be able to empathize with the joys and sorrows and struggles that others also experience.

I believe it's O.K. to stop our distracting busyness for a few minutes during autumn days to watch the yellowing leaves quietly helicopter downward to the still-green grass, to become aware of the changes in the cricket sounds, to sense the changing smells. I believe it's O.K. to notice how the autumn rains seem to accentuate the colors, to pause and appreciate the nearby hillside turning from lush greens to oranges, reds and yellows, then to a kind of rusty brown and finally to a gray-brown in expectation of the first winter snows. It's O.K. to watch a curled yellow-orange leaf softly drift with the current of a clear and shallow creek. I believe it's O.K. to sit on a backyard slope with one's aging feline companion and, as Virginia Stem Owens put it, watch "the woods happen for one afternoon."[20]

In the Stillness Also Is the Voice

Be still, and know that I am God!
—Psalm 46: 10

And behold, the Lord passed by, and a great and strong wind rent the mountains, and broke in pieces the rocks before the Lord, but the Lord was not in the wind; and after the wind an earthquake, but the Lord was not in the earthquake; and after the earthquake a fire, but the Lord was not in the fire; and after the fire a still small voice.
—I Kings 19: 11-12

Each time he read those biblical passages, vivid images of past personal experiences came to mind, experiences that, to him, were very spiritual, inviting him to think deeply about life: "What is life really all about?"... "How is one to live life?"... "What is really important in life?"... "Who am I?"

As a young boy growing up on a farm, he found that one of the best ways to sort out his thoughts after a day at school was to walk to the back of the field just before sunset and sit on a disk plow which had been left there many years before. From that vantage point, apart from the world, and in the silence that characterizes that time of the day, he would become lost in his thoughts. In these "disk-plow meditations," he began to feel that there must be some kind of meaning or purpose to life, to *his* life. Further, he began to wonder why he had these kinds of thoughts, and he wondered whether or not other kids his age also struggled with such issues.

Be still, and know that I am God!

It was the year 1964, and he was a brand new second lieutenant attending infantry officer training at Fort Benning, Georgia. On this particular day, the student officers were on a map-reading exercise somewhere in the pines. As he followed his compass to the next checkpoint, he stopped to get his bearings. Becoming aware of his immediate surroundings, he noticed he was standing in a dry creek bed. Suddenly he felt an overwhelming, soul-piercing stillness. The only movement among those towering pines was that of a tiny bird flitting from branch to limb in a bush that grew out of the creek bank.

. . .and after the fire a still small voice.

In the summer of 1971 he would write:

> It was Sunday morning in Big Bend National Park. We had stopped at a small ranger station, and I had started talking to a traveller from California. It was then that I noticed the total absence of sound. The pauses in our conversation were punctuated by an absolute silence that touched deep into the soul. No city noises. No airplanes. No wind. Nothing. Nothing but rugged semiarid country interrupted by majestic peaks and cliffs in the distance.

He would go on to characterize that profoundly spiritual experience as a sermon of silence, more profound than many spoken sermons!

Be still, and know that I am God!

For five years he worked in Washington, D.C., most of that time in the Pentagon. He lived in an apartment in Arlington, and drove to and from work in that mechanized madness that is part of the Washington scene during rush hour. The last few months he worked in Washington, he was transferred to a location much nearer his apartment than the Pentagon, a location within walking distance. A whole new world was opened up to him as he went to and from work each day. The walk was not nearly as wearing as the driving had been; he was able to notice the sounds of the birds and crickets, the aroma of the flowers: things that one is not aware of when fighting the traffic closed up in a car! The pace was much slower, much gentler, and more sane. One day as he walked through one of the entrances, he cut across what was a kind of sunken parklike area on the grounds. It was a whole different universe: quiet, still–a tiny wilderness of bushes, trees, flowers, birds and squirrels in the midst of all of that largely unnoticed human activity. The noise of the perpetual gridlock seemed so distant. There was a profound peacefulness in the midst of chaotic movement. For a few minutes each day as he walked through that area, there was a kind of calling of the spirit, a time of reflection and meditation, a chance to open to, even to wonder about, the truly important things of life.

. . .and after the fire a still small voice.

Years later, he was in training to be a hospital chaplain in a large cancer center in Texas. One day, after several weeks of ministering among cancer patients, he felt a desperate need to "withdraw to a place apart"–to get away from the pain and hurt–and he walked out into the vast parking lot between the several hospitals that make up that medical center. As he strolled through the rows and rows of cars, he noticed and picked up one of the few autumn-colored leaves lying next to a tree. It was tiny compared to the towering buildings, and probably unnoticed by the people walking by. But for him, during such a heavy time, it was exactly what he needed. He turned, with renewed inner strength, and walked back into being with those who struggled.

Be still, and know that I am God!

There are many times of "disk-plow meditations" in our lives when God is known–

not in the singing of great hymns,
not in the reading of Scripture,
not in the great and powerful voice from the pulpit,
not in the spoken prayer,
not in the bustle of church fellowship,
but in the *stillness*, in the still small voice.

Veterans Day Reflections

In November we celebrate Veterans Day. It was originally known as Armistice Day ("the 11th hour of the 11th day of the 11th month" of 1918 when the guns fell silent in Europe) to commemorate the end of World War I. That was the war that was going to end all wars. However, it turned out to be the war to end all illusions that the twentieth century would be a grand and glorious time of peace and human progress. Thus, over the coming decades, many more people would become veterans.

Many times, weather and time permitting, when I was assigned a funeral at the National Cemetery, I would go a little early to walk among the rows and rows of gray-white stones, reading names and dates—no, more accurately, reading stories, life stories of once living, breathing human beings. There is a Floyd Alexander, born in 1892, who served as a wagoneer with the 10th Cavalry: Buffalo soldier. There is a George Preston Murphy who died in June 1945: no other information. There is a Joseph Ridge from Missouri who was a bugler in World War I, and a Charles Adams who served as a cook in the Spanish American War (1898). There is an Aaron S. McCarter, who served with the 16th Infantry Regiment in the Mexican War: that was 1846-1848, even before the Civil War! Then there is Mary L. Pahmahmie, who served in the Army Nurse Corps during World War II: she was born in 1905, the same year as my mother. Who were these people? What did they think about life? Did they think life was worth the effort? Were they loved by someone? Did anyone show up for their funeral? Those stones represent unique and significant human stories, stories that include hope and despair, laughter and tears, victories and defeats, loneliness and companionship, high drama and routine boredom, dreams and disappointments, acceptance and rejection.

As I remember those veterans, I am reminded of other kinds of veterans: the mothers and fathers of those who served, who anxiously and prayerfully awaited their loved one's return, fearful of that knock at the door, the wives and sweethearts hoping against hope for their loved one's return.

There was a night a long time ago on the other side of the earth in the midst of seemingly endless rice paddies that I sat listening to radio transmissions that spoke of people frantically attempting to save the life of a young Naval officer, and I became painfully aware that just at that moment some mother had just lost a son, some wife had just become a widow, some sweetheart had just lost a lover or some child had just lost her father. That person at home also had become a veteran, a casualty of war. At such times I suspect that these veterans suffer as much, if not more, than those of us who have served in the military.

As we remember those who have served in the armed forces, let us not fall into the trap of glorifying the wars they fought in (I suspect that ultimately nations tend to glorify wars and warriors in order to justify and to live with what they have done to other human beings), for war is a cruel and vicious experience that not only destroys physical bodies, but also wounds and distorts the human spirit. And it wounds not only those who serve in uniform, but also the innocent and most vulnerable who are swept up into the maelstrom.

Let us all work toward a time, however distant and

seemingly unrealistic and naive, when people shall truly "beat their swords into plowshares and their spears into pruning hooks; nation shall not lift up sword against nation, neither shall they learn war any more..." (Is. 2: 4). Let us work toward a time when the *last* veteran shall be laid to rest amidst those rows and rows of gray-white stones.

A Very Personal Reason for Thanksgiving

It seems that an essential part of our human spirituality is to feel we are accepted by and acceptable to significant others, to feel we are loved and capable of loving. To feel thus is to feel a kind of spiritual security and stability out of which we can relate to the rest of the world. I was again reminded of this when I came across an old letter I had written to my family attempting to relate the memories of childhood Thanksgivings back in Texas.

> There were Thanksgivings past . . . when our family would go down to our (maternal) grandparents' ranch on the other side of Lowake and spend the day. It was a special time: not only was it a day off from school, but it was the front door to the Christmas season (the season which brought forth all of the Lionel train displays in the toy departments–Heaven! After a check of things cooking in the kitchen (grandma always had my brother and me inspect the homegrown turkey roasting in the oven when we arrived) and quick hellos to kinfolk, we kids were outside–down to the "branch," into the pasture or out front to "knock flies" with cousins. Only the cry, "Dinner's ready! You all come on in!" brought a halt to our activities. There was a wash pan and a nearby bucket of water on the gallery (a screened-in, L-shaped porch where much life took place) where we washed our hands before going into the dining room (on colder Thanksgivings, a fire roared in the cylindrical coal oil

stove in the middle of the room). Once inside, there was always some confusion as places to sit were designated. There was a slight (and awkward) pause before one of the grown-ups asked one or more of us kids to return thanks. And, then came the *food!* To hear the men talk on the gallery (in conversations which we kids felt irrelevant to reality and to the exciting things of life) about the poor crops just harvested, one would think we were starving; to see the food that made its way around the table one would think we were rich. We were rich, not in money, but in life, in living, in spirit. There was turkey, dressing, potatoes —two kinds, mashed and whole (grandpa didn't like mashed)—homegrown green beans, gravy, corn and cranberries ("Yecch!"). When all had eaten until they talked about being stuffed, the dessert came in the form of pies and cakes (an aunt made delicious chocolate cakes with icing smothered in pecans). No one ever seemed too stuffed to have at least one piece, and some of us kids were known to have room for multiple servings! After dinner, people drifted into various rooms to talk in quiet conversations, to take a nap or to do the dishes." If we kids were told to lie down for awhile, a good place was a northwest bedroom with a window facing the southern November sun. One was awakened later to the aroma of lunch coffee cooking. Lunch meant pies, cakes, cookies, coffee (for the grown-ups) or tea (iced), leftover turkey and dressing. Again, we stuffed, and then uncles and aunts and cousins began getting ready to go home: had to "get the eggs" and close the chickens up for the night; the cows needed to be fed; Neal had to study his English—the reasons for leaving (at that particular time of the day) were standard (as if we would stay there forever if we couldn't come up with a good reason for going home). Once all the pie plates and cake savers were collected and the people were ready, the "administrative" conversations began: where to have Christmas (our families alternated holiday meals); "What are you going to do about that sick cow?"; "Will you come pick up the trailer?"—all of those things that wait until the pressure of the last minute to be said. The sun would be setting among the mesquite trees as we drove up the caliche road to the highway, and then home.

This letter of Thanksgiving memories, written years ago, was an attempt to share some of the supportive, nurturing environment in which I grew up. Even, and especially, after I experienced the devastation of polio and the resulting facial paralysis in 1952 (at age 11), I never doubted that I was loved and accepted just as I was by those persons who were most significant in my life. It was this kind of upbringing that provided the spiritual security and stability which laid the foundation that would help carry me through the severest of life's storms as I continued my journey through the years. Further, I am certain that my understanding of God as a loving, caring, nurturing, forgiving God, rather than a harsh, judgmental, angry, vindictive judge, has much to do with this loving family environment. For this kind of heritage, I have a very personal and very great reason for thanksgiving!

December Reflections

Retired General Harold Moore, in the prologue of his book *We Were Soldiers Once . . . And Young* about the First Cavalry Division's fierce and bitter battles with the North Vietnamese in the Ia Drang Valley of South Viet Nam in 1965, wrote:

> . . . This story also stands as tribute to the hundreds of young men of the . . . People's Army of Vietnam who died by our hand in that place. They, too, fought and died bravely. They were a worthy enemy. We who killed them pray that their bones were recovered from that wild, desolate place where we left them, and taken home for decent and honorable burial.[21]

It is in the light of this moving and powerful attempt at reconciliation between two former enemies that I, as a veteran working among veterans, am reminded that December is not only Christmas month but Pearl Harbor month and Battle of the Bulge month. These two wartime experiences evoke painful and bitter memories, especially for many World War II veterans—and not only the military veterans of that war, but also those other veterans, the mothers, fathers, wives, sweethearts, children back home.

But then, we are all veterans ("one who has had experience in some field"), if not of military wars, then of the battles of life, especially those experiences which have wounded us deeply. In this, I am aware of how we humans can easily make a career out of chronic bitterness and vindictiveness over something that happened to us years ago—especially painful experiences of feeling

wronged by another person. I've been there! Such bitterness can give us a perverse sense of self-righteous energy that drives our lives—and by which we identify ourselves. It can be a way to feel good about ourselves—or at least better than others—as we pass judgment and condemnation on others. It can also be a way of justifying our personal failures as well as our personal prejudices.

However, I am also aware that such attitudes are a kind of spiritual cancer that can and do slowly eat away at our personal integrity. These attitudes keep us from being all that God wants us to be and stunt our spiritual growth. Perpetuation of personal grudges, be they against our former wartime enemies or against some individual or group we believe has wronged us, only makes us less human.

Can we veterans, particularly during this holiday season, be challenged to see the connection between our attitudes toward our former and current enemies and the meaning of the Christmas story? My personal understanding of the significance and the message of that long-ago manger is that it calls us to think anew and to see and relate to others in a radically different way. The desire and need for vengeance and the continued cultivation of resentment is to be replaced by an ongoing effort at forgiveness and reconciliation. We learn that abundant life occurs when we attempt to move beyond destructive hatred, continuing resentment, chronic bitterness, corrosive vindictiveness—and instead seek understanding and reconciliation: when we persevere in the struggle to overcome evil with good.

Perhaps true and lasting healing from our psychospiritual wounds begins only when we are able to move beyond the need for bitterness and revenge—when we, like General Moore, are able to appreciate the pain and the humanity of the former "enemy." Perhaps there is some connection between what I am attempting to say and what Andrew Greeley once said of Christmas:

Still
Jesus was crazy.

He came into the world with the nutty idea that human beings could love one another . . . .

Peace on earth indeed.
Maybe Jesus should have stayed home.
He was wrong. We cannot love one another.
The best we can do is keep the levels of hatred
low enough so we don't exterminate one another before we all die of pollution or the world gets fouled up in the ultimate rush hour traffic jam . . . .

It was a great idea, of course.
Too bad it didn't work . . . .

Still . . .

What if He wasn't crazy? What if He was right?
What if it is possible to love one another?
What if the lion can lie down with the lamb?
What if Arab and Jew, Protestant and Catholic,
black and white, young and old, male and female
can love one another without fear, without hatred,
without death and destruction? . . .

What if the crib scene is what the world is really all about and everything else is phony?
What would it be like if Jesus knew the way things really were?
What if life does triumph over death, light over darkness, good over evil, love over hate, comedy over tragedy?[22]

This Thing Called Christmas

What is Christmas all about, anyway? To attempt, in a few paragraphs, to answer that question, to write down the final word about the meaning and significance of Christmas, would be rather presumptuous of me. At best, I can only share some personal thoughts from the perspective of this particular milepost in my life journey, realizing that my perspectives will change as the journey continues.

I would have to preface any discussion of Christmas with some observations.

First, I want to suggest that *Christmas tends to be a very personal time* (even in the midst of family gatherings, the crowds, and festivities) in that no two of us experiences this season the same. One person once supposedly said that no two of us experiences the sunset the same. I believe that this also applies to our experience of Christmas.

Secondly, *none of us has two Christmases that are alike*. We have lived through the experiences of 365 days since the last Christmas, and these experiences, which continually shape our feelings and moods, our attitudes and perspectives, affect the way we experience each Christmas. For example, my Christmas at home in Texas in 1965 was far different from my Christmas in Viet Nam in 1966! We may have lost a loved one, gained or lost a job, gotten married or divorced, given birth to a child, or experienced a significant illness or disability between Christmases. In other words, none of us is the same person that last Christmas saw!

Thirdly, *just because it is a holiday season doesn't change other things that are going on in our lives* and in the tumultuous world around us! Even if we would like to somehow suspend all of the painful experiences for a few weeks in order to celebrate the birth of the Prince of Peace, this does not happen! Life, with all of its bumps and grinds, (war, turmoil, illness, oppression, death of loved ones) goes on, even at Christmas time.

Keeping these observations in mind, I would like to suggest that the celebration of Christmas is, to a very large extent, *a celebration of God's love for each of us* as individuals. The birth of the Christ Child is a message–a reminder–that despite all of our sins, hang-ups and weaknesses, God loves us. One of the messages of Christmas is: "You are worth the effort! You are of personal intrinsic value!"

Christmas is also a celebration of the human endeavor, the human journey, the human experiment. For many people, life can become a kind of routine drudgery; it can become, at times, even a burden. Between the headaches and the heartaches, there is often not much room left for the good times, the happy times, times of celebration. Then, along comes Christmas, and even in our greatest discouragement and frustration, we can feel a sense of hope that there is something good, after all, about our existence. We sense that even our worst, most painful experiences can somehow be redeemed into something positive and contributive–contributive not only to our own life but to the lives of others. When we have just about given up on the human race–on ourselves–along comes Christmas to remind us that there is Someone (some Force) greater than we can possibly comprehend who had (and has) enough faith in the potential of humans to relate to each other in love that this Someone sent is really all about. This Someone shows us what the bottom line really is, what is really of lasting and eternal value. Along comes Christmas to renew our hope that, in spite of our failings and fears, perhaps, just perhaps, the human experiment might work out after all! And, all of this can give us the courage, the energy, to keep on keeping on, even when common sense tells us there is no use. Thus, Christmas becomes a time to celebrate the human journey.

Finally, I would suggest that celebrating Christmas is *celebrating* the opportunity for a new spiritual rebirth every year. It is a reminder that God gives us a second (and third, and fourth, and, if necessary, a ten-thousandth) chance in life. As Eugene Kennedy, in *The Pain of Being Human*, said:

> The Christian who lives by the Spirit knows that there is no end to his need to begin again but he also knows that God's promises are the guarantee that he always can begin again. That is what the resurrected life of the Spirit looks like. In living it, the Christian is a source of hope and a real sign of salvation for the whole world.[23]

Christmas is a primary reminder that we have this gift from God: the miracle of being allowed—even encouraged!—to start all over again in our spiritual quests. Our past sins and failings and mistakes and defeats need not destroy our relationship with God or separate us from God's love. They need not weigh us down in guilt and shame and worthlessness, destroying our future, causing a wasted life. Christmas is a reminder that we can truly be born anew, not just once, but many times, as we struggle through life! And, herein lies hope!

Notes

1. Eugene Kennedy, *The Joy of Being Human* (Garden City, NY: Doubleday & Co: An Image Book, 1974), p. 9.

2. Loren Eiseley, *All the Strange Hours: The Excavation of a Life* (New York: Charles Scribner's Sons, 1975), p. 12.

3. John MacQuarrie, *The Humility of God* (Philadelphia: The Westminster Press, 1978), p. 49.

4. This list, composed by the Reverend Cornie G. Remple of Winnipeg, Manitoba, Canada, is from *The Pilgrim's Log*, Volume 26, September 24, 1983, Issue 32, of the Pilgrim United Church of Christ, Wichita Kansas.

5. Harvey Pottoff, *God and the Celebration of Life* (Chicago: Rand McNally & Co., 1969), p. 239.

6. L. Harold DeWolf, *A Theology of the Living Church* (New York: Harper & Row, 1968), p. 165.

7. Mark Sheldon, from *The Upper Room*, November 17, 1992, p. 20.

8. George Roberson, from *The Upper Room*, May 21, 1993, p. 24.

9. Mary Klipston, from *The Upper Room*, June 23, 1993, p. 59.

10. Gordon Poteat, *The Interpreter's Bible*, Volume XII (Nashville: Abington Press, 1957) p. 34.

11. Peter Singer, "A Covenant for the Ark?" *Life and Meaning: A Reader*, ed. Oswald Hanfling (Cambridget, MA: The Open University, Basil Blackwell, Inc., 1987), p. 152.

12. Harvey Pottoff, *God and the Celebration of Life*, p. 28.

13. Loren Eiseley, *The Star Thrower* (New York: Harcourt Brace Javanovich, 1978), p. 181.

14. Loren Eiseley, *The Immense Journey* (New York: Vintage Books, 1957), p. 13.

15. Sue Lennon, from *The Upper Room*, Volume 59, Number 4, September-October 1993, p. 27.

16. Wendy Wright, "Memories of Now," *Weavings: A Journal of the Christian Spiritual Life*, Volume X, Number 3 May/June 1995, p. 13.

17. T.H. Watkins, *The Great Depression: America in the 1930's* (Boston: Little, Brown & Co., 1993), p. 127.

Errata Sheet

The top line on page 101 is missing:

this Child into the world to show us what the good life

Reference numbers 5 and 12 on page 102 should read:

Harvey Potthoff

The Author

Robert W. Janek, a hospital chaplain, was born in Fort Worth, Texas, adopted by a cotton farmer and his schoolteacher wife, and grew up with his older brother Neal on Lipan Flats near San Angelo, Texas. Upon graduating from college, he spent four years as an officer in the army, including one year in Viet Nam. He then worked for the Defense Intelligence Agency in Washington, D.C., for five years before attending seminary in Colorado. He is ordained in the Unity of the Brethren and in the United Church of Christ denominations.

His wife Jena is a piano teacher. They have one grown son, Daryl.

18. *Twenty-Four Hours a Day* (Center City, MN: Hazeldon Press, 1975), May 28.

19. Eugene Kennedy, *The Joy of Being Human*, p. 245.

20. Virginia Stem Owens, *A Feast of Families* (New York: Macmillan Publishing Company, 1983), p. 32.

21. Harold G. Moore, *We Were Soldiers Once* (New York: Random House, 1992), p. xvi.

22. Andrew Greeley, "Christmas Is Really a Humbug," *The Chicago Tribune*, December 25, 1973. Reprinted in Mark Link, S.J., *The Merriest Christmas* (Niles, IL: Argus Communications, 1974), p. 100.

23. Eugene Kennedy, *The Pain of Being Human* (Garden City, NY: Doubleday & Co: An Image Book., 1972), p. 277.